creatures of the sea

The Crab

Other titles in the series:

creatures of the sea

The Crab

Kris Hirschmann

KIDHAVEN
PRESS™

THOMSON

™

GALE

San Diego • Detroit • New York • San Francisco • Cleveland
New Haven, Conn. • Waterville, Maine • London • Munich

For more information, contact
KidHaven Press
27500 Drake Rd.
Farmington Hills, MI 48331-3535
Or you can visit our Internet site at http://www.gale.com

LIBRARY OF CONGRESS CATALOGING-IN-PUBLICATION DATA

Hirschmann, Kris, 1967–
  Crabs / by Kris Hirschmann.
    v. cm.—(Creatures of the sea)
Includes bibliographical references.
Summary: Examines types, environments, feeding, and life cycles of the crab.
Contents: Looking at crabs—Crabs at home —Finding food, becoming
food—Life cycle.
  ISBN 0-7377-1554-5 (hardback : alk. paper)
  1. Crabs—Juvenile literature. [1. Crabs.] I. Title.
  QL444 .M33 H56 2004
  595 .3'86—dc21

2003001633

Printed in China

Table of Contents

Classifying Crabs

Crabs belong to a group of animals called **arthropods**. More than nine hundred thousand known species (about three-quarters of the animals on Earth) belong to the arthropod group. This group includes insects, spiders, centipedes, and many other animals besides crabs. Arthropods have jointed legs and no backbones. They also have **exoskeletons**, a hard outer covering that surrounds and supports the body, instead of internal bones.

Within the arthropod group, crabs are part of a smaller group called the crustaceans. Lobsters, shrimps, and crayfish are also members of the crustacean group, which includes about forty thousand animal species. Different types of crustaceans are very different in size and shape. All crustaceans, however, have certain common features, including exoskeletons and two pairs of **antennae**, long sensory organs on the head.

There are about forty-five hundred species of crabs. This is just a small percentage of the world's crustaceans and an even smaller percentage of the world's arthropods. Yet crabs have a special place in this group of animals: The largest crabs are the world's biggest arthropods. This means they are the biggest crustaceans, too. Indeed, crabs are giants compared to wood lice and other small crustaceans. With their large bodies, crabs are sure to be noticed wherever they appear.

A girl finds a kelp crab at low tide.

1

Looking at Crabs

Crabs come in many different shapes and sizes. The smallest are the tiny pea crabs, whose shells are less than one-quarter inch across. The largest are the giant spider crabs of Japan, which measure as much as twelve feet from leg tip to leg tip. All other crabs fall somewhere between these extremes.

Although crabs' sizes vary, all crabs share certain traits. These shared traits make crabs easy to identify. They also give crabs everything they need to survive in their home environment.

Three Main Parts

Like all crustaceans, crabs have three main body sections. The three sections are the head (front section), the thorax (middle section), and the abdomen (rear section). The crab's head and thorax are joined into one part called the **cephalothorax.** In most species, the cephalothorax is broad and flattened.

The crab's abdomen is attached to the rear of the cephalothorax. The crab folds its abdomen tightly against the bottom of the cephalothorax and tucks it into a groove that is the exact size and shape of the abdomen. The abdomen fits so snugly into this groove that it does not look like a separate body part. It just looks like an outlined shape on the crab's underside. This outlined shape

A scuba diver looks at a giant spider crab, which is one of the largest crabs in the world.

Hermit crabs adopt other animals' abandoned shells.

may vary between males and females of the same species. Often females' abdomens are broad and rounded, while males' abdomens are narrow and pointy.

The hermit crab's abdomen is different from that of most crabs. This crab has a long, soft abdomen that does not fold under its cephalothorax. Instead, the hermit crab tucks its abdomen into the abandoned shells of snails and other sea creatures. These shells protect the hermit crab's soft belly.

Legs and Limbs

Crabs have five pairs of legs, all of which are attached to the thorax. The front two legs are the largest.

They are also the most dangerous, since they end in pinching claws. A leg that ends in a pinching claw is called a **cheliped,** and the pincer itself is called a **chela.** In some species, both chelae are the same size. In other species, one chela is larger than the other. The fiddler crab, for example, has one huge chela and one small one.

The other eight legs are smaller and are used mostly for walking. In most species, all of the walking

The fiddler crab uses its cheliped to make noise to warn other crabs in their burrows that they are in danger.

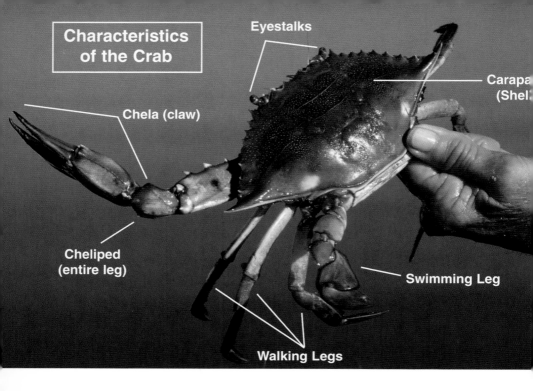

Characteristics of the Crab

Eyestalks

Carapace (Shell)

Chela (claw)

Cheliped (entire leg)

Swimming Leg

Walking Legs

legs end in points. In species that can swim, such as the blue crab and the lady crab, the back two legs are usually shaped like paddles. The green crab, which lives on the north Atlantic coast of the United States, is an exception. This swimmer has pointed back legs instead of paddles.

In addition to their ten legs, crabs also have five pairs of limbs on the head. Two pairs act as antennae. Two other pairs are used to stuff food into the mouth, and one pair is used for chewing.

A Hard Covering

All of the crab's body parts are covered by a hard shell called an exoskeleton. The exoskeleton protects and supports the soft parts of the crab's body.

The crab's cephalothorax is covered by a thick part of the exoskeleton called the **carapace.** The carapace is usually smooth, with the front edge shaped into a series of bumps or spines. The number and shape of these bumps and spines varies from species to species.

A crab's legs are also covered with hard material. The exoskeleton covering the crab's legs is not nearly as thick as the material covering the cephalothorax. It is especially thin at the joints, where the exoskeleton must be flexible so the crab can move its legs.

Breathing

Although the exoskeleton covers and protects the crab's body, it also has many holes that allow water, food, and other materials to pass in and out. Two of these holes are for breathing. The breathing holes are found near the crab's front legs. These holes let water enter the crab's **gills.** The gills then take oxygen from the water and release carbon dioxide from the crab's body. Crabs use **gill bailers,** tiny paddle-like organs on the jaws, to push water into the breathing holes and over the gills. After the gills have absorbed the water's oxygen and released carbon dioxide, the used water exits the crab's body through another pair of holes over the mouth.

Some crabs do not have to be underwater to breathe. Many types of crabs can store water inside their bodies, then leave the ocean. They use their gill bailers to blow air over the stored water and keep it full of oxygen. Some crabs even breathe air instead of water. However, there are fewer air-breathing crabs than water-breathing crabs.

Sensing the World

The breathing holes are not the only openings in the crab's exoskeleton. The exoskeleton also has many holes that let the crab's sensory organs poke out. Sensory organs let crabs see, smell, feel, and sense the world in many other ways.

Eyes are two of the crab's most important sensory organs. A crab's eyes are found on the ends of two long stalks at the front of the carapace. Crabs have compound eyes, which means the surface of each eye is made up of hundreds of tiny lenses. Each lens gathers just a little piece of an image. In the crab's brain, all these little bits are put together to create a complete image.

Two sets of antennae are also found at the front of the carapace. These antennae detect smells and tastes. They also contain organs that give the crab its sense of balance and tell the crab whether it is right side up or upside down.

Touch is another important sense. Crabs feel the world with stiff bristles that poke out through tiny holes in the exoskeleton. Although a crab has sensory bristles all over its body, most of the bristles are found on the walking legs and chelipeds. As the crab moves around, the bristles bump into things. This is

The eyes of a hermit crab are on movable stalks that allow it to see in every direction, even behind it.

the way the crab feels rocks, ocean currents, and other things in its environment.

Crabs can also sense vibrations in the water. These vibrations tell crabs about objects and animals moving in the distance. A crab can feel a swimming predator, for instance, or a nearby crab clacking its chelae. This information, along with the senses of vision, smell, taste, and touch, gives crabs everything they need to be successful in their everyday lives.

2

Crabs at Home

Crabs are common around the world and are found mostly in the water. Most water-dwelling crabs make their homes in the Earth's oceans. They are found everywhere, from cold polar waters to tropical seas. Some water-dwelling crab species live in freshwater environments, such as lakes and rivers, but there are far fewer freshwater than saltwater crabs.

Although most crabs live in the water, some species can be found on land. Beaches, rain forests, and other damp areas make good homes for land-dwelling crabs.

In the sea or on the land, crabs choose a variety of homes. Rocks, mud, sand, tide pools, burrows, and even inside other animals are just a few of the many places crabs can be found.

Down in the Sea

The Earth's oceans are full of crabs. Crabs can be found in every ocean on Earth and at every depth, from coastal shallows and tide pools to the deepest regions of the sea. Crabs are so widespread, in fact, that they are sometimes called "spiders of the sea." This nickname suggests that crabs are just as common in the water as spiders are on land.

Different crabs have different ranges. Some types of crabs are found around the world, while others stay in smaller areas. Box crabs, for example, live in many

The Australian blue swimming crab spreads its claws wide to defend itself.

different oceans, while the giant Japanese crab lives only off the coast of Japan.

Within the ocean environment, crabs have many different types of homes. Some crabs, including box crabs and decorator crabs, live in tide pools. Other crabs, including the rock crab of New England, squeeze themselves into cracks between rocks lying on the ocean floor. Blue crabs and some other species bury themselves in the mud. Some species, including coral crabs and some hermit crabs, choose to live on coral reefs. And the vent crab makes its home in the black depths of the ocean near deepwater vents, underwater volcanoes that spew superheated water and other materials.

Shore Dwellers

Some types of crabs live on the water's edge instead of in the water. These crabs, called shore dwellers, stay close to the ocean or another body of water but seldom enter it.

Ghost crabs and sand crabs are probably the best-known shore dwellers. These crabs are fairly small. Their carapaces measure just an inch or two across. They live in burrows on sandy beaches around the world. They often wander away from their burrows, but they skitter back home at the first sign of danger. To run, these crabs rise up on their leg tips and scoot sideways over the sand.

Fiddler crabs are another well-known shore-dwelling species. Fiddler crabs dig burrows in mud

Although you may see a ghost crab during the day, you are more likely to see them at night when they are more active.

flats or sand marshes near the edges of rivers. These crabs tend to live close to each other, so a large mud flat or marsh may be home to thousands of fiddler crabs.

The Sally Lightfoot crab also lives at the ocean's edge. Instead of digging a burrow, however, this crab clings to rocks along the water line. Sally Lightfoot crabs have a powerful grip and are known for their ability to cling to even the slipperiest wave-battered rocks.

The stone crab is yet another shore dweller. Stone crabs live in mud holes or between rocks along the borders of creeks. People sometimes catch stone crabs by poking rods into their holes. After a stone crab grabs the rod with its chelae, it can be pulled from its hiding place.

Living on Dry Land

Some types of crabs make their homes on dry land, far from the ocean or any other body of water. As a group, these crabs are often called simply "land crabs." Most species of land crabs live underground.

The bright colors of the sally lightfoot crab make it easy to see on the beach.

This land crab rests on a cactus.

Land crabs are so well adapted to living on the land instead of in the sea that they breathe air instead of water. However, they still need to live where conditions are damp. Land crabs therefore are most commonly found in the tropics, where the weather is humid. Also, most land crabs are active at night, when there is no hot sun to dry them out.

The coconut crab is an interesting land dweller. This crab is large. It sometimes measures more than three feet from leg tip to leg tip and weighs up to thirty-five pounds. It lives in burrows and often climbs trees. Coconut crabs are sometimes called "robber crabs" because they have been known to steal people's belongings and drag the items back to their burrows.

Some Unusual Homes

A few types of crabs have unusual homes. Among the strangest homes are those of the pea crabs. These tiny animals live inside the shells of mussels, oysters, and other shellfish. They can also be found inside the tube-shaped lairs of certain sea worms. Pea crabs do not seem to bother their hosts at all. They live quietly, gathering scraps of food that are dropped when their hosts feed.

Porcelain crabs can also live closely with other animals. Some of these crabs make their homes among the stinging tentacles of sea anemones, plant-like creatures with hundreds or thousands of flexible, waving arms. The anemones do not sting the porcelain crab because its shell protects it. Animals without shells, however, could be hurt by the anemone. For this reason, fish and other unprotected creatures seldom bother the porcelain crab.

Some porcelain crabs live among the tentacles of sea anemone.

Hermit crabs also have unusual homes. These crabs do not settle in one place, as most crabs do. Instead, they carry their houses with them. A hermit crab pokes its long, soft abdomen into the empty shell of a snail or another sea creature and then carries the shell everywhere it goes. When a hermit crab needs a safe hiding place, it simply pulls the front part of its body into the shell and blocks the shell's opening with one chela.

Because crabs have adopted so many different living conditions, they can be found in both watery and dry environments all over the world. The crab's ability to adapt has made it one of the world's most successful animals.

3

Finding Food, Becoming Food

Crabs eat a wide variety of foods. Some crabs are carnivores. This means they eat only other animals. Other crabs are herbivores and eat only plants. Most crabs, however, will eat just about anything they can find. Plants, dead animals, live animals, and food scraps left by other animals all make good meals for a hungry crab.

Crabs are also hunted by many other animals. Therefore, they have developed many defenses to keep themselves safe from attackers. With a little luck, a crab will be able to find meals over a long period of time without becoming a meal itself.

Finding Food

Crabs that eat anything are known as scavengers. Most crabs fall into this category. Scavenging crabs constantly roam their home areas looking for things to eat. Dead fish, slow-moving worms, rotten fruit, fallen leaves, and just about any other animal or plant material are tasty treats for a scavenger.

Some crabs that can move quickly prefer to hunt live animals. Crabs that catch living meals are called predators. The green crab, a swimmer that eats mostly shellfish, is one example of a predatory crab. Most other swimming crabs are also speedy enough to catch and eat fish, shrimp, and other fast-moving creatures.

A hermit crab crawls inside a coconut. Coconut meat is one of the hermit crab's favorite foods.

Filter feeding is another way that crabs can find a meal. Crabs that collect food in this way have fringed antennae or other limbs that they wave through the water. They do this to catch tiny bits of food to eat. Porcelain crabs, coral hermit crabs, and pea crabs are just a few examples of filter feeders.

Some crabs are specialists that prefer one type of food over all others. The coconut crab falls into this category. This crab's favorite food is the white inner flesh of coconuts. A coconut crab uses its strong chelae to crack a coconut's thick shell and reach the food inside.

Grabbing and Eating

Before a crab can eat anything, it must grab it. The chelae are the crab's main grabbing tools. These claws are hinged so they can open and close easily. And the inner edges are jagged for gripping and tearing food. The chelae are also very strong. They can close tight, allowing a crab to get a good grip on its meal.

For hunting crabs, the chelae serve as powerful weapons. The claws' jagged edges are good for grasping fish and other slippery prey and for tearing the animals' flesh into bite-sized chunks once they are caught.

The chelae are also important to filter feeders and scavengers. Filter feeders use their chelae to scrape particles off their antennae. Scavengers use

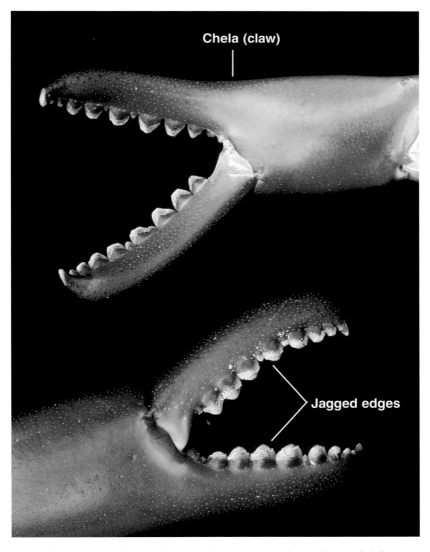

Chela (claw)

Jagged edges

The chela, or claw, of a crab act as a hand would for a human.

their chelae to pick up and tear the food they find lying around.

All crabs use their chelae to place food into their mouths. Once in the mouth, the food is torn into smaller pieces by limbs located on the crab's head. The shredded food then passes into the stomach, where it is digested.

Crab Self-Defense

A crab's chelae are not used only for eating. They are also used for defense. Many animals, including birds, octopuses, rays, sharks, and eels, enjoy eating crabs and will grab them whenever possible. When threatened by a predator, a crab raises its chelae and waves them. This is the crab's way of telling other creatures to back off. If the predator attacks anyway, the crab will pinch it.

Of course, it is better for a crab if it never has to face a predator in the first place. Therefore crabs do their best not to be noticed. Hiding is the easiest way to do this. Crabs may bury themselves in the sand, squeeze their bodies between rocks, or conceal themselves in seaweed beds. By staying out of sight, a crab reduces its chance of becoming a meal.

Some crabs have body colors that blend with the background and keep them hidden. A crab with protective colors is said to be camouflaged. The hairy porcelain crab, for example, has a dark, rough body that perfectly matches its rocky home. Ghost crabs and sand crabs are also well camouflaged. These beach dwellers may be pale yellow or another color that makes them hard to spot against a sandy surface.

If all of these defenses fail and a crab is grabbed by a leg, it can leave the leg behind. Special breaking points let a crab drop its limbs without doing itself any serious harm. The missing body parts will grow back over time.

Unusual Defenses

Some crabs use unusual tricks to keep themselves hidden. Some types of spider crabs, for example, conceal themselves by covering their carapaces with seaweed, sponges, and other materials. These crabs seem to know what types of materials blend best with their surroundings. If they move from one place to

A spider crab hides in a sea anemone.

Crew members bring a crab trap on to the Pacific Wind Catcher Processor.

another, they drop their old coverings and pick up new ones that better match their new environment.

Decorator crabs use a similar method to hide themselves. These crabs use their chelae to snip off pieces of sea sponges large enough to cover their carapaces. Then they use their rear walking legs to hold the sponges over their backs like umbrellas. This hides their bodies from view.

Some hermit crabs protect themselves by planting sea anemones on their shells. Once attached, the anemones go everywhere the hermit crab goes. Predators cannot attack the hermit crab without being stung by the anemones' tentacles, so they usually leave the crab alone.

Boxer crabs also use anemones to protect themselves. Instead of planting the anemones on their backs, however, these crabs hold one anemone in each chela. If a predator approaches, the crab waves the anemones to scare it off.

Crabs and Humans

All of a crab's defenses cannot protect it against the biggest predators of all: humans. Fishermen around the world catch millions of pounds of crabs each year and sell them as food. Blue crabs, king crabs, green crabs, and Dungeness crabs are just a few species that often wind up in grocery stores and on restaurant plates.

So far, human fishing activities have not pushed any crab species to the point of extinction. This is partly because laws regulate the amount and the size of crabs people may catch. In some areas, however, overfishing of crabs has dramatically reduced the crab population. In Maryland's Chesapeake Bay, for example, there was five times as much crabbing activity in the year 2000 as there had been fifteen years before. But the total blue crab catch remained about the same. This is because the blue crab population had shrunk, so the crabs were much harder to catch.

Still, the crab population in Maryland and other areas around the world is large enough to be safe from extinction. With laws in place to protect crabs, even the most hunted species will roam the world's oceans far into the future.

chapter 24

Life Cycle

Different species of crabs have different life expectancies. Most crabs live just two or three years. A few species, however, have much longer lives. If they do not get sick, injured, or eaten, Dungeness crabs live as many as eight years, stone crabs may live ten years, and king crabs may reach fourteen years of age.

During its life span, no matter how long or short, every crab goes through a cycle that includes birth, growth, reproduction, and death. This cycle produces new crabs and keeps the world crab population healthy and stable.

Crab Larvae

Crabs start their lives as tiny **larvae** called **zoeae** that hatch from eggs. A zoea has a long, thin abdomen, big round eyes, and a long spike on the back of its head. It looks more like a shrimp than a crab.

As soon as it hatches, a zoea floats away on the ocean currents and becomes part of the plankton, a population of very small plants and animals that floats near the water's surface. Within the plankton, the zoea eats as many tiny creatures and plants as possible and tries to avoid being eaten itself. If it survives, the zoea grows quickly. In about a month it becomes heavy enough to sink from the plankton and fall to the ocean floor.

On the ocean floor, the zoea changes into another larval form called a **megalops.** The megalops

A close look at the crab zoeae.

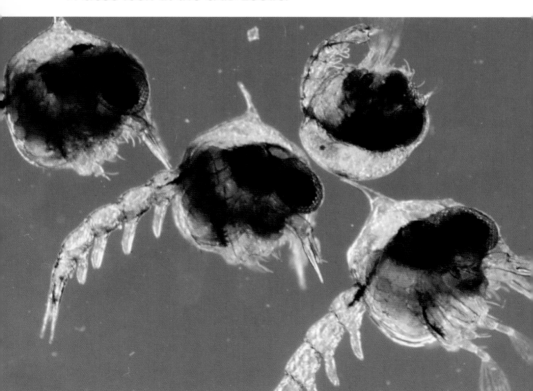

has huge eyes,   long abdomen, and swimming legs. It is bigger than the zoea, and it looks more like a crab than the zoea did. However, the megalops is still far from its adult form.

The megalops stage lasts about two months. After that period the larva goes through another change. It now looks like a tiny crab. The little crab immediately adopts an adult lifestyle and starts eating. If it manages to stay away from predators, the crab will eventually grow to its full size. This process might take as much as a year, depending on the species.

Molting

Like adult crabs, zoeae and megalops larvae have hard exoskeletons. An exoskeleton cannot change size, so crabs must shed their exoskeletons every now and then in order to grow. This process is called **molting.** Once the old exoskeleton has been shed, the crab grows a new, larger one.

Molting happens naturally as a crab's soft inner body gets bigger. The crab's growing body puts pressure on the exoskeleton until it finally cracks around the edge of the carapace. The crab then crawls out of the crack and leaves the old shell behind.

This is a dangerous time for a crab. Without its exoskeleton, the crab is too soft to walk or eat. Also, it has no protection from predators. For these reasons, crabs look for safe hiding places when they are getting ready to molt.

A blue crab (pictured) is vulnerable to predators until it is finished shedding its shell.

After molting, a crab immediately gulps in water to inflate its soft body. It does this so that the new shell it is growing will be as large as possible. The bigger the shell, the longer it will be before the crab has to molt again. After a few days the crab's outer layer hardens into a new, larger exoskeleton. Carrying its new suit of protective armor, the crab comes out of hiding and goes back to its normal routine.

The number of times a crab molts in its lifetime varies from species to species. Some crabs molt only a few times. Others molt dozens of times over the course of their lives. In all species, young crabs molt more often than older ones.

Mating

After a number of molts, a crab is an adult. It is now ready to mate and create baby crabs of its own.

To begin the mating process, a male crab must first attract a female. Different species have different ways of doing this. The fiddler crab, for example, waves its chelae to get a female's attention. The blue crab dances in front of a female with its claws outstretched. And the hermit crab simply grabs a female and holds on tight.

Once a male finds a mate, he climbs onto her back and grips her snugly. The female loosens her abdomen. The male then deposits a material called sperm into pockets beneath the female's abdomen. This material will be used to fertilize the female's eggs and start the growing process. The female stores the sperm inside her body until she is ready to lay her eggs.

After mating, most crabs separate immediately. Some crabs, however, stay together for several days.

Blue crabs and shore crabs are two types of crabs that do this. These crabs mate while the female's body is still soft after a molting. Once the males have released their sperm, they carry the female beneath their own bodies until her shell has hardened. In this way the female is safe from predators while she is soft and vulnerable.

Producing Eggs

Depending on the species, it may take up to a couple of months after mating for a female crab to lay her eggs. When she is ready, a female lays millions of eggs

The larger male velvet swimming crab will guard the female beneath him until they mate.

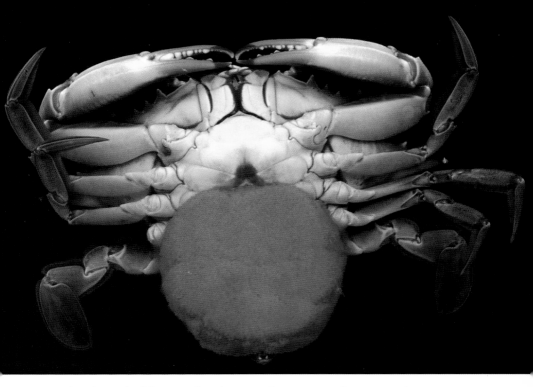

The female blue crab, shown above carrying eggs in an orange mass, can produce up to 8 million eggs.

at once. She uses the stored sperm to fertilize the eggs as they leave her body. She also produces a sticky substance that she uses to cement the eggs together into one large clump.

A crab's eggs need to stay wet in order to develop properly. This is no problem for water-dwelling crabs. Land and shore crabs, however, must make an extra effort to keep their eggs moist. Some of these crabs make frequent trips to the water to dunk their eggs. Others leave their dry homes temporarily and live in the ocean or another body of water until the eggs hatch.

The red crabs of Christmas Island in the Indian Ocean make this move in a spectacular way. Once each year, millions of these crabs leave the woods and march to the water's edge to mate and lay their eggs. They move together in thick streams, climbing down cliffs and over or around anything that might be in their way. This migration can last as long as eighteen days. It has been described by scientists as one of the wonders of the natural world.

Once all her eggs have been laid, a female uses her abdomen to hold them tightly against her thorax. The egg mass bulges out around the edges of the abdomen. A female in this condition is said to be "in berry." She will hold the eggs against her body until they hatch. Depending on the species, this process can take anywhere from a couple of weeks to several months. When the zoeae emerge, they float away to become part of the plankton, and a new cycle of life begins.

Glossary

antennae: Sensory organs on a crab's head.

arthropods: A group of animals with exoskeletons and jointed legs.

carapace: The hard shell that covers a crab's cephalothorax.

cephalothorax: A crab's head and thorax together.

chela: A pinching claw.

cheliped: A leg that ends in a pinching claw.

exoskeleton: A hard outer skeleton that surrounds and protects a crab's body.

gill bailers: Paddlelike organs that push water into a crab's breathing holes.

gills: Organs that release carbon dioxide and take in oxygen.

larvae (or one larva): The name for newly hatched crabs until they change into their adult form.

megalops: The second larval stage of a crab.

molting: Shedding the exoskeleton.

zoeae (or one zoea): The first larval stage of crabs.

For Further Exploration

Books

Jim Capossela, *How to Catch Crabs by the Bushel! The Manual of Sport Crabbing.* Tarrytown, NY: Northeast Sportsman's Press, 1982. Includes plenty of tips on catching and cooking crabs.

Philippe De Vosjoli, *The Care of Land Hermit Crabs.* Escondido, CA: Advanced Vivarium Systems, 1999. A complete pet owner's guide to taking care of captive hermit crabs.

Edward R. Ricciuti, *Crustaceans.* Woodbridge, CT: Blackbirch Press, 1994. Read all about the crustacean family. Includes chapters on senses, metabolism, food chains, and more.

Websites

Crabs (www.kidskonnect.com). This page includes links to information about many different types of crabs, including blue crabs, fiddler crabs, hermit crabs, and more.

Dr. Darren's World of Crabs (www.brachyura. fsnet.co.uk). Includes a wealth of crab information and pictures as well as crab puzzles, racing games, movie posters, and other fun stuff.

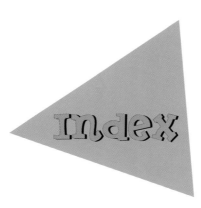

Index

picture credits

about the author

Kris Hirschmann has written more than seventy books for children. She is the president of The Word-shop, a business that provides a wide variety of writing and editorial services. She holds a bachelor's degree in psychology from Dartmouth College in Hanover, New Hampshire. Hirschmann lives just outside of Orlando, Florida, with her husband, Michael, and her daughter, Nikki.